WHAT WE STAND FOR

DO SOMETHING FOR OTHERS

the kids' book of
CITIZENSHIP

ANDERS HANSON

CONSULTING EDITOR, DIANE CRAIG, M.A./READING SPECIALIST

Super Sandcastle

An Imprint of Abdo Publishing
www.abdopublishing.com

visit us at www.abdopublishing.com

Published by Abdo Publishing, a division of ABDO, PO Box 398166, Minneapolis, Minnesota 55439.
Copyright © 2015 by Abdo Consulting Group, Inc. International copyrights reserved in all countries.
No part of this book may be reproduced in any form without written permission from the publisher.
Super SandCastle™ is a trademark and logo of Abdo Publishing.

Printed in the United States of America, North Mankato, Minnesota
062014
092014

THIS BOOK CONTAINS
RECYCLED MATERIALS

Editor: Liz Salzmann
Content Developer: Nancy Tuminelly
Cover and Interior Design and Production: Anders Hanson, Mighty Media, Inc.
Photo Credits: Shutterstock

Library of Congress Cataloging-in-Publication Data

Hanson, Anders, 1980-
  Do something for others : the kids' book of citizenship / Anders Hanson ; Consulting Editor, Diane Craig,
M.A., Reading Specialist.
     pages cm. -- (What we stand for)
  ISBN 978-1-62403-292-9
1. Civics--Juvenile literature. 2. Citizenship--Juvenile literature. I. Title.
  JK1759.H226 2015
  323.6--dc23
                              2013041828

Super SandCastle™ books are created by a team of professional educators, reading specialists, and content developers around five essential components—phonemic awareness, phonics, vocabulary, text comprehension, and fluency—to assist young readers as they develop reading skills and strategies and increase their general knowledge. All books are written, reviewed, and leveled for guided reading, early reading intervention, and Accelerated Reader® programs for use in shared, guided, and independent reading and writing activities to support a balanced approach to literacy instruction.

CONTENTS

WHAT IS
CITIZENSHIP?

Citizenship is being
part of a community.

A country is a large
community. Every country
has its own flag.

Different types
of people
can be citizens
of the same
community.

Cassie is at
school. All the
students live in
the same town.

Citizens have rights.

Adults have the right to live and work in their country.
They have the right to vote. They can run for office too.

Citizens also have duties.

Adults have many duties. They need to obey laws.
They need to pay taxes. They may need to be on a **jury**!

WHAT CAN YOU DO?

How can kids be good citizens?

FOLLOW THE RULES.

The rules are there because most people agree on them.

Ms. Foster's class is at a museum. The guide says one of the rules is to talk quietly.

BE RESPECTFUL.

Treat people the way you want to be treated.

Jeremy listens to his grandfather. He tells Jeremy what school was like when he was young.

TAKE CARE
OF THE
ENVIRONMENT.

Plant trees for cleaner air.

Don't waste water or power.

Recycle.

Angie has a red shovel. She
helps her mom plant a tree.

BE TOLERANT OF OTHERS.

People may look or act differently than you.

Try getting to know them. They won't seem so strange!

HELP OTHERS WHEN YOU CAN.

Helping other people makes them happy! It also makes you happy!

Shawn helps his little brother with his bike helmet.

WHAT WILL YOU DO?

What is one thing you can do to be a better citizen?

GLOSSARY

ENVIRONMENT – nature and everything in it, such as the land, sea, and air.

JURY – a group of people chosen to attend a trial and decide whether the accused person is innocent or guilty.

TOLERANT – showing respect for or acceptance of behaviors or beliefs that are different from your own.